WRITING

# *Writing Home*

—*—

HUGO WILLIAMS

Oxford New York
OXFORD UNIVERSITY PRESS
1985

*Oxford University Press, Walton Street, Oxford OX2 6DP*
*Oxford New York Toronto*
*Delhi Bombay Calcutta Madras Karachi*
*Kuala Lumpur Singapore Hong Kong Tokyo*
*Nairobi Dar es Salaam Cape Town*
*Melbourne Auckland*
*and associated companies in*
*Beirut Berlin Ibadan Mexico City Nicosia*

*Oxford is a trade mark of Oxford University Press*



*First published 1985 by Oxford University Press*



*British Library Cataloguing in Publication Data*
*Williams, Hugo*
*Writing home.—(Oxford paperbacks)*
*I. Title*
*821'.914 PR6073.I432*
*ISBN 0–19–211970–2*

*Library of Congress Cataloging in Publication Data*
*Williams, Hugo, 1942–*
*Writing home.*
*(Oxford paperbacks)*
*I. Title.*
*PR6073.I432W5 1985 821'.914 85–4901*
*ISBN 0–19–211970–2 (pbk.)*

*Set by Promenade Graphics Ltd.*
*Printed in Great Britain by*
*J. W. Arrowsmith Ltd, Bristol*

*To my Mother*

# ACKNOWLEDGEMENTS

Some of these poems first appeared in the *London Review of Books*, the *New Statesman*, the *Times Literary Supplement*, the *London Magazine*, the *New Review*, the *Listener*, *Firebird*, the *Observer*, *PEN New Poetry 1* (Quartet), the *Fiction Magazine*, and *Poetry* (Chicago).

# CONTENTS

# At Least a Hundred Words

What shall we say in our letters home?
That we're perfectly all right?
That we stand on the playground with red faces
and our hair sticking up?
That we give people Chinese burns?
Mr Ray, standing in the entrance to the lavatories
with his clip-board and pen,
turned us round by our heads
and gave us a boot up the arse.
We can't put that in our letters home
because Mr Ray is taking letter-writing.
He sits in his master's chair
winding the propeller of his balsa wood aeroplane
with a glue-caked index finger
and looking straight ahead.
RESULTS OF THE MATCH, DESCRIPTION OF THE FLOODS,
THE LECTURE ON KENYA, UGANDA AND TANGANYIKA
WITH COLOUR SLIDES AND HEADDRESSES.
We have to write at least a hundred words
to the satisfaction of Mr Ray
before we can go in to tea.
We're not allowed to put 'And then this happened',
'And then that happened',
so I put up my hand to ask if we count the 'ands'.
Mr Ray lets go the propeller of his Prestwick 'Pioneer'
and it unwinds with a long drawn-out sigh.
He'd rather be out overflying
enemy territory on remote
than 'ministering to the natives' in backward C4.
He was shot down in World War One or World War
Two, he forgets,
but it didn't do him a damn bit of harm.
It made a man of him.
He goes and stands in the corner near the door

and offers up his usual prayer:
*'One two three four five six seven*
*God give me strength to carry on'.*
While his back is turned
I roll a marble along the groove in the top of my desk
till it drops through the inkwell
onto the track I've made for it inside. I can hear it
travelling round the system of books
and rulers: a tip-balance, then a spiral,
then a thirty year gap as it falls through
the dust-hole into my waiting hand.

# Just Another Day

When you were young
you came downstairs in the middle of the night
and saw the living room.
The furniture lay about your feet.
The carpet had been folded back
where it met the skirting board.

You opened the front door
and stood for a moment on the step.
Little pieces of metal
shone in the asphalt on the road.
The chimnies were pot-bellied apostles
preaching to the stars.

You cleared your throat, or coughed,
and the dawn chorus started up—
excited by an item of news
which might have been you,
or might have been just another day.
You stood there for a moment, listening.

# Before the War

'You should have been there then', they tell you,
the girls who were there themselves.
'Before the war,
your father was the kind of man
to take you, on the spur of a telegram,
to one of those Continental casinos
where they keep the curtains drawn
all summer: white ties and Sidney Bechet,
gardenias on a breakfast tray.
You'd follow the road map south
in someone's aeroplane,
putting down in a field while it was light.
Oh, those were the days all right
and the nights too for someone like your father.'

Then you mourn the fact once more
that you missed knowing him then,
that you hardly recognize this man
who somehow jumped the gun
and started ahead of you. It isn't fair,
but there's nothing to be done. The casinos are dead
and the nights are drawing in.
Though you follow the road map south
on the spur of a lifetime
you'll never catch up with the fun
and he won't be back for you.
You're strung out like runners
across the world, losing ground,
in a race that began when you were born.

# A Walking Gentleman

I started very slowly,
being rude to everybody
and going home early
without really knowing why.
I carried on that way
till my father died
and allowed me to grow my hair.
I didn't want to any more.
I came through a side door,
my hands slightly raised,
as if whatever was going on
needed lifting by me.
I bought a clove carnation
in Moyses Stevens
and cut the sepals off
and forced the whole thing
through my buttonhole
till it lay flat against the lapel
like a brooch, not a bouquet.
I walked all the way up Piccadilly
to the top of the Haymarket,
stopping every so often.
Surely Scott's is somewhere near here?
I can't see it any more.
My feet are hurting me.

# Waiting To Go On

I turned the pages slowly, listening for the car,
till my father was young again, a soldier,
or throwing back his head
on slicked back Derby Days before the war.
I stared at all that fame and handsomeness
and thought they were the same.
Good looks were everything where I came from.
They made you laugh. They made you have a tan.
They made you speak with conviction.
'Such a nice young man!' my mother used to say.
'So good looking!' I didn't agree with her,
but I searched my face for signs of excellence,
turning up my collar in the long mirror on the stairs
and flourishing a dress sword at myself:
'Hugh Williams, even more handsome in Regency!'
The sound of wheels on the drive
meant I had about one minute
to put everything back where I'd found it
and come downstairs as myself.

# Tipping My Chair

I shivered in 1958. I caught a glimpse
of money working and I shut my eyes.
I was a love-sick crammer-candidate, reading
poetry under the desk in History,
wondering how to go about my life.
'Write a novel!' said my father.
'Put everything in! Sell the film rights for a fortune!
Sit up straight!' I sat there, filleting
a chestnut leaf in my lap, not listening.
I wanted to do nothing, urgently.

At his desk, in his dressing-gown,
among compliant womenfolk, he seemed
too masterful, too horrified by me.
He banged the table if I tipped my chair.
He couldn't stand my hair. One day,
struggling with a chestnut leaf, I fell over backwards
or the chair-leg broke. I didn't care any more
if poetry was easier than prose. I lay there
in the ruins of a perfectly good chair
and opened my eyes. I knew what I didn't want to do.

At his desk, in his dressing-room, among
these photographs of my father in costume,
I wonder how to go about his life.
Put everything in? The bankruptcy? The hell?
The little cork-and-leather theatrical
'lifts' he used to wear? The blacking for his hair?
Or again: leave everything out? Do nothing,
tip my chair back and stare at him for once,
my lip trembling at forty?
My father bangs the table: 'Sit up straight!'

# A Little While Longer

My father stands at an angle
to the Church of St Ethelburga in the City,
the divorcees' church.
My mother hangs back,
shielding her eyes from the flashes.
She twists her new ring,
while my father explains to reporters
how something unwinds in mid-air—
a marriage perhaps,
or could it be a googly?
His knuckles show white
on the officer's swagger stick
which he's holding like a kite reel.
*Why clench thy fists, O little one?*
*Thy mother's near and sure there's none*
*would wish to fight thee.*
The reporters laugh uneasily,
remembering to mention
the children of a previous marriage,
their ages and places of birth.
They've asked him to smile
and he's twisted his moustache for them.
His seedy, civilian best man
tries to pull him away to the reception.

# An Actor's War

## Tunisia, 1943

'It is difficult to assess the value of the part played by the organisation known as Phantom during this stage of our operations in North Africa.'

—*Official History of the Second World War*

Before the British public
I was once a leading man.
Now behind a British private
I just follow, if I can.

—Hugh Williams

*March*

*Well, here we are in our Tropical Kit—*
*shirts and shorts and little black toques,*
*looking like a lot of hikers or cyclists*
*with dead bluebells on the handlebars.*
*It seems we have at last discovered a place*
*where it is impossible to spend money. What a pity*
*that it should be a rather muddy wadi*
*in Tunisia, where whisky is prohibited by God.*
*How sorry I am that I ever said an unkind word*
*about the Palmer's Arms. In my nostalgia*
*it seems the very Elysium of Alcohol.*
*I can imagine you in about an hour*
*pattering round to meet your beaux.*
*The last couple of days I've realized with a bang*
*what an appalling time this bloody war has been on.*
*Three and a half years last night*
*since we walked out of the stage door of the Queen's Theatre*
*into the Queen's Westminsters.*
*What good times we had. But it all seems*
*a long time ago, looking back, doesn't it?*

*April*

*Early morning—or what in happier times*
*was late at night. Strong and sweet black coffee,*
*laced with the last little drop out of my flask,*
*has reminded me of that stuff they used to serve*
*on fire inside a coconut at The Beachcomber*
*to put the finishing touches to a Zombie.*
*I'm still floundering in the work here.*
*I lie awake sometimes wondering if my map*
*is marked correctly. I lose notebooks*
*and have to rely on little bits of paper.*
*Benzedrine tablets, please. Chemist next to the Pavilion.*
*A kiss and a lump of chocolate for Hugo*
*for being able to walk.*
*Please God he never has to march.*

*May*

*It's all very green down here at the moment—*
*lots of wild flowers and lots of your gum trees*
*with their barks hanging down like tattered lingerie.*
*I saw a stork flying and heard a lark singing*
*as though he were over Goodwood racecourse*
*on that wonderful day when Epigram won the Cup*
*and you won me. The villages look like those*
*in Provence and the milestones with little red tops*
*make me long for the days to come*
*when you and I are scuttling down the Route Bleue*
*in search of sunshine and eights and nines.*
*Having taken trouble all one's life to seek pleasure,*
*to find now that delights are down to a canvas bath*
*taken with one's legs hanging over the side in a bucket,*
*is strange, though no doubt good for one.*
*I dare say I shall be pretty bloody exquisite*
*for quite some time after the war—silks and lotions*
*and long sessions at the barber*
*and never again will a red carnation be made to last*

*from lunchtime until the following dawn.*
*When the war is over I intend no longer*
*to practise this foolish and half-hearted method*
*of letting money slip through my fingers.*
*I intend in future to allow it to pour*
*in great torrents from my pockets.*
*Don't be alarmed. This is only the talk of a man*
*with mosquito lotion on his face and hands*
*and anti-louse powder in the seams of his clothes,*
*who drinks his highly-medicated morning tea*
*from a tin mug with shaving soap round the rim*
*and uses gum boots for bedroom slippers.*

*June*

*Writing by our Mediterranean now, but the wrong bank.*
*The same sunshine and azure sea, a few of the same*
*flowers and trees and the purple bougainvillea,*
*but there it ends. Enough to make one want more—*
*a bottle cooling in a pool,*
*a yellow bathing dress drying on a rock.*
*Perhaps if we fight on we shall arrive in a country*
*where there is something fit to drink.*
*How pleasant to be advancing through the Côte d'Or*
*with one's water bottle filled with Pouilly.*
*Instead of which we're stuck in this blasted cork forest*
*learning to kill flies.*
*Sometimes it seems we love England*
*more than each other, the things we do for her.*
*I wonder if, when it's over, we'll be glad.*
*Or shall we think I was a fool to sacrifice so much?*
*Oh God, we'll be glad, won't we? I don't know.*
*Not on this damned dust hurricane I don't.*
*But if you love me I shan't care.*
*You and Hugo have a coating of desert on your faces.*
*I must wipe you.*

*July*

*The battle—if one can dignify such a shambles—*
*is closed in this sector and there is an atmosphere*
*of emptying the ashtrays and counting the broken glasses.*
*Churchill arrived to address the First Army*
*in the Roman Amphitheatre at Carthage.*
*He looked like a Disney or Beatrix Potter creature*
*and spoke without his teeth. Cigar, V-sign, all the tricks,*
*and I thought of that day outside the Palace*
*with Chamberlain smiling peace with honour*
*and we kidded ourselves there was a chance—*
*two little suckers so in love*
*and so longing for a tranquil sunny life.*

*August*

*How's my boy? Shirts and trousers!*
*Poor little Hawes and Curtis. Another year or so*
*and our accounts will be getting muddled*
*and I shall find myself getting involved*
*in white waistcoats I've never seen.*
*Tell him to pay cash. Go and tell him now.*
*The thought terrifies me.*
*Have been harassed lately by the old divided duties—*
*the only part of the war I can honestly say*
*has been bloody. Maybe the cinema racket*
*gives one the wrong impression of one's worth,*
*but I sometimes feel I'd be better employed at Denham*
*as Captain Daring R.N. than housekeeping for Phantom.*
*Stupid, for one must do one or the other*
*and not attempt both as I have done.*
*Had a letter from the Income Tax*
*asking for some quite ridiculous sum.*
*Next time you see Lil tell her to write and say*
*I'm unlikely to be traceable*
*until quite some time after the war, if then.*
*I think when I die I should like my ashes*

*blown through the keyhole of the Treasury*
*in lieu of further payments.*
*My wages here are roughly what it used to cost me*
*to look after my top hat before the war.*
*Flog it, by all means. I can't see that kind of thing*
*being any use after the war, unless it's for comedy.*
*Did some Shakespeare at the Hospital Concert*
*the other night and was nervous as a cat.*
*God knows what a London first night will be like*
*with all the knockers out front, waiting and hoping.*
*I doubt if I'll make it. Sometimes I really doubt it.*
*I'll probably run screaming from the theatre*
*just as they call the first quarter.*
*Tell the girls to keep on with Puck and the First Fairy*
*as I shall want to see it when I come home.*

*September*

*Had a deadly exercise down on the plain last week*
*and the blasted Arabs stole my lavatory seat.*
*Medals should be given for exercises, not campaigns.*
*One would have the Spartan Star for Needless Discomfort*
*in the face of Overwhelming Boredom.*
*I had to give a cheque for £48 to Peter Baker*
*and I doubt there's that much in my account.*
*Now he's going home by air because of an appendix*
*and taking the cheque with him.*
*I couldn't be sorrier to do this to you once again,*
*but his appendix took me by suprise, as it did him.*
*Tell Connie I must have a picture before Christmas.*

*October*

*Every known kind of delay and disappointment*
*has attended us and I am filled with a sulky despair*
*and a general loathing for mankind.*
*People are so bored they have started growing*
*and shaving off moustaches, a sure sign*

*of utter moral decay. I have luckily made friends*
*with a little fellow who keeps me supplied*
*with a sufficiency of Algerian brandy,*
*so I expect the major part of my waking life*
*to be spent in pain and hangover.*
*Added to all other horrors,*
*Christmas Theatricals have cropped up,*
*which really has crowned my ultimate unhappiness.*
*Perhaps if I tell you that after*
*an hour and a half of forceful argument*
*I have just succeeded in squashing an idea*
*to produce an abbreviated version of Midsummer Night's*
*Dream*
*by the end of the week—without wigs, costumes,*
*stage or lighting and only one copy of the play,*
*you will appreciate the nervous exhaustion I suffer.*
*The idea of acting is rich. Not for a line of this letter*
*have I avoided making those aimless*
*slightly crazy-looking gestures to remove the flies.*
*I have a mug of tea and there must be thirty round the brim.*
*I can kill them now by flicking them,*
*as opposed to banging oneself all over.*
*I think they must be slower down here,*
*for I can't believe that I am quicker.*

# As I Went To Sleep

At last he was coming home, whoever he was.
In a couple of weeks we'd be hearing the telephone
and Nanny's boyfriend would be going home to America.

I put my ear to the humming telephone poles
and intercepted my father's messages.
I sent him messages in my prayers,

then Nanny's boyfriend moved my cot out into the hall
and slipped some chewing gum under my pillow
to keep my mouth shut. The smell of spearmint

made my mouth water. As I went to sleep
I could hear them calling one another's name
as if they were already miles apart.

# Tangerines

'Before the war' was once-upon-a-time
in 1947. I had to peer through cigarette smoke
to see my parents in black and white
lounging on zebra skins, while doormen stood by doors
in pale grey uniforms.

I wished I was alive before the war
when Tony and Mike rode their bicycles into the lake,
but after the war was where I had to stay,
upstairs in the nursery, with Nanny
and the rocking-horse. It sounded more fun
to dance all night and fly to France for breakfast.
But after the war I had to go to bed.

In my prisoner's pyjamas I looked through
bannisters into that polished, pre-war place
where my parents lived. If I leaned out
I could see the elephant's foot
tortured with shooting sticks
and a round mirror which bulged from time to time
with hats and coats and shouts,
then emptied like a bath.

Every summer my parents got in the car
and drove back through the war to the South of France.
I longed to go with them, but I was stuck
in 1948 with Nanny Monkenbeck.

They sent me sword-shaped eucalyptus leaves
and purple, pre-war flowers, pressed
between the pages of my first letters. One year
a box of tangerines arrived for me from France.
I hid behind the sofa in my parents' bedroom,
eating my way south to join them.

# Slow Train

My father let the leather window-strap
slip through his fingers and I smelt the sea.
He was showing me gun emplacements
to stop me feeling train-sick
on our first holiday after the war.
I clutched my new bucket in two lifeless hands,
excited by the blockhouse
which had exploded, killing everyone.
We went over a bridge he had guarded
and he lit two cigarettes and threw them down
to some soldiers cutting barbed wire.
He said there was something fast for me
in the guard's van, if I could hang on.
I sat there, staring at one of the holes
in the window-strap, imagining death
as a sort of surprise for men in uniform.
'I-think-I-can-I-think-I-can'
the train was supposed to be saying
as we came to Dungeness Lighthouse in the dark,
but I didn't think I could.
When we started going backwards, I was glad.

# New Coat, Last Chance

I wore a coat like this
when they rescued me from the plot
of my first adventure.

I was climbing the weir with my dog.
'Don't move!' shouted my governess
from the prow of a motorboat.

I washed my hands in the vestry,
but the smell of oilskin
stayed on my fingers in church.

My disgrace comes back to me now
as I turn up the collar
in the long mirror of this shop.

'Don't move!' whispers my governess.
Her goggles freeze me in my tracks.
My feet slither.

Smells remember us as we were then—
half fact, half fiction—
trying on different clothes.

They race ahead of us like spaniels,
turning and waiting by a river
for their masters to come true.

# Walking Out Of The Room Backwards

Out of work at fifty, smoking fifty a day,
my father wore his sheepskin coat
and went to auditions
for the first time in his life.
I watched in horror from my bedroom window
as he missed the bus to London
in full view of the house opposite.
'If it weren't for you and the children',
he told my mother from his bed,
'I'd never get up in the morning.'

He wasn't amused
when I burst in on his sleep
with a head hollowed out of a turnip
swinging from a broom. There were cigarette burns
like bullet-holes in his pyjamas.
I saw his bad foot
sticking out from under the bedclothes
because he was 'broke'
and I thought my father was dying.
I wanted to make him laugh, but I got it wrong
and only frightened myself.

The future stands behind us, holding ready
a chloroform-soaked handkerchief.
The past stretches ahead, into which we stare,
as into the eyes of our parents
on their wedding day—
shouting something from the crowd
or waving things on sticks
to make them look at us. To punish me,
or amuse his theatrical friends,
my father made me walk out of the room backwards,
bowing and saying, 'Goodnight, my liege'.

# Leaving School

I was eight when I set out into the world
wearing a grey flannel suit.
I had my own suitcase.
I thought it was going to be fun.
I wasn't listening
when everything was explained to us in the Library,
so the first night I didn't have any sheets.
The headmaster's wife told me
to think of the timetable as a game of 'Battleships'.
She found me walking around upstairs
wearing the wrong shoes.

I liked all the waiting we had to do at school,
but I didn't like the work.
I could only read certain things
which I'd read before, like the Billy Goat Gruff books,
but they didn't have them there.
They had the Beacon Series.
I said 'I don't know,'
then I started saying nothing.
Every day my name was read out
because I'd forgotten to hang something up.

I was so far away from home I used to forget things.
I forgot how to get undressed.
You're supposed to take off your shirt and vest
after you've put on your pyjama bottoms.
When the headmaster's wife came round for Inspection
I was fully dressed again, ready for bed.
She had my toothbrush in her hand
and she wanted to know why it was dry.
I was miles away, with my suitcase, leaving school.

# Scratches

My mother scratched the soles of my shoes
to stop me slipping
when I went away to school.

I didn't think a few scratches
with a pair of scissors
was going to be enough.

I was walking on ice,
my arms stretched out.
I didn't know where I was going.

Her scratches soon disappeared
when I started sliding
down those polished corridors.

I slid into class.
I slid across the hall into the changing-room.
I never slipped up.

I learnt how to skate along with an aeroplane
or a car, looking ordinary,
pretending to have fun.

I learnt how long a run I needed
to carry me as far as the gym
in time for Absences.

I turned as I went,
my arms stretched out to catch the door jamb
as I went flying past.

# Heroes of the Sub-Plot

Look at us, cursed heroes of the sub-plot,
twisting our faces into plaintive masks
over the footlights—terror, desire and glee.
For we are lost, as usual at this hour,
in a wood near the front of the stage—
cuckolds and clowns and palace functionaries,
rolling our eyes to pass the time for you
with one or two approved cross purposes.
See—we have put on character make-up
to distract you from the sound of scenery
being shifted behind our backs. The principals
are waiting in the wings: all too soon
our leading man will make the winding sign
to end our moment balanced in the light.
We smudge our eye-shadow with our tears.

# When Will His Stupid Head Remember?

Mr Ray stood behind me in History,
waiting for me to make a slip.
I had to write out the Kings and Queens
of England, in reverse order, with dates. I put,
'William I, 1087–1066'. I could smell the aeroplane glue
on his fingers as he took hold of my ear.
I stood in the corner near the insect case,
remembering my bike. I had the John Bull
Puncture Repair Kit in my pocket: glass paper,
rubber solution, patches, chalk and grater,
spare valves. I was 'riding dead'—
freewheeling downhill with my arms folded
and my eyes shut, looking Mr Ray in the eye.
Everytime I looked round he added a minute to my
sentence.

Mr Ray held his red Biro Minor like a modelling knife
to write reports. He drew a wooden spoon.
'I found it hard to keep my temper
with this feeble and incompetent creature.
He was always last to find his place
and most of his questions had been answered
five minutes before . . .' I called my father 'sir'
when he opened the envelope and shouted.
I was practising stage-falls from my bike
in the fading spotlight of summer lawns,
remembering the smell of aeroplane glue and inkwells
with a shiver down my spine. The beginning of term
was creeping up on me again. Every time I looked round
Mr Ray was standing there, stockstill.

# A Letter To My Parents

There is quite a lot of news from this front.
I got hit in the face, but I am all right now.
How are you? How is the play?
A little dog called Bobby ran out into the road
and was run over by a car.
I am sorry this is in pencil, but I am upstairs
lying down. I am in the same room as last term
but my bed is next to my old one
and bang next to the door.
Roberts is sleeping in my old bed.
We are going to have a gang, so we sign our name in blood.
We have to have sunray treatment
which seems a complete waste of time.
We had a lecture on the Headhunters of Borneo.
The Headhunters are in the literal sense.
They cut off your head
and cut off all your hair
and play football with your skull.
Or else they bash up all your brains and pour hot sand
in through your neck, until it shrinks
and they paint it blue.
Then afterwards we played charades with the man.
We had to do the word pill.
Then we had to do the word oh. (Pillow)
There were two old people in India
and the door had blown open.
'First to speak closes the door', said the man.
Then in the morning the woman had to speak.
'Woman, you have spoken. Close the door.'
I will tell you about charades in more detail
when you come down.
Could you bring some decorations with you?
And one or two of your plays that you don't really want?
I am sending the going out days for you to fill in.
Apparently there is a map, or you could ask.

# Shelf Life

1.
Above our beds
the little wooden shelf
with one support
was like a crucifix
offering up
its hairbrush, Bible,
family photograph
for trial by mockery.

We lay in its shadow
on summer nights,
denying everything,
hearing only
the impossible high catches
for the older boys,
their famous surnames
calling them to glory.

2.
Why did we take
the bed-making competition
so seriously?
We were only nine.
We measured our turndowns
with a ruler.
We used a protractor
to fix the angle of our
hospital corners
at forty-five degrees.

Our shelves were identical.
Our Bibles lay
on their sides, facing in.
Our hairbrushes lay on their backs
with a comb stuck in them.
If anyone's hairbrush had a handle
they had to hide it
in their dressing-gown
and borrow a proper one
for the competition.

In the centre of our shelves
stood our photo-frame,
a difficult area
that couldn't be tidied away
or forgiven. By the time we had
solved the problem
of our counterpane
our parents were looking
straight past one another
into opposite corners of the room.

3.
Their smiles were
lost on us
and ours on them,
as if they were still
waving goodbye to the wrong
upstairs window
from the car.
In their long absence,
our double photo-frame
was a bedtime
story-book,
propped open like a trap
at the pictures.

We said to ourselves,
'Brothers and sisters
have I none,
but this man's father
is my father's son.
Who am I?'—
holding our fingers
on our father's
encouraging smile
and repeating it
over to ourselves
till we started
to lose our place.

4.
I knew it wasn't my father
who was bankrupt and poor.
He had a war.
He had a scar.
He was on Famous Film Star
Cigarette Cards
with Janet Gaynor.
It couldn't be my father
who hit the registrar
and had to be bound over for a year
to keep the peace,
so who were they talking about
in the newspaper?
If he was famous,
why hadn't I heard of him?

He looked uncertain
in the signed
photograph on my shelf
that was attracting
too much attention
for my own good.

His hair was perfection.
His eyes were fixed on the horizon
where something vaguely
troublesome was going on
behind my back.
The smoke from his cigarette
had been touched in
against a background
of pleated satin.

5.
I found his name
in the Library *Who's Who*
and tore the page out
hoping it would say.
I memorized dozens
of forgotten films and plays
to prove my father
innocent of bankruptcy.
His brief biography
was followed by a personal note:
'Clubs: none, Sports: none,
Hobbies: none.
Address: c/o *Spotlight*.'

6.
I tried to explain
that the German
bubble-car
in the photograph
of our house
was part of
a Spitfire
my father had flown
in the war.

The swastikas
on my blanket
were ancient
symbols of fortune
the other way round.

I sat in bed
tracing the faces
of my parents
on lavatory paper.
Riddles and smut
poured from their lips
in my defence,
but the evidence
was attached to
a blind-cord.
Up it flew,
hoisting my shit-
stained underpants
into full view.

# A Collection of Literature

*My Dear Williams,*
*I am sorry to have to bother you on this score,*
*but I feel it is my duty to let you know*
*what has come to light today. Under separate cover*
*I am sending you a collection of literature*
*which I have taken from Hugo.*

*This morning he left under his mattress*
*a copy of 'The Man'. When taxed with this,*
*he said he had bought it on Boxmoor Station*
*on his day out. He admitted that he had passed it on*
*to several other boys and during the course*
*of investigations it transpired*
*that he had a lot of other magazines of this type,*
*which he says he brought from home.*

*At first I thought it might have been a piece of*
*childish stupidity on his part,*
*but when all these other magazines came to light*
*I realized that it went deeper.*

*I am very surprised that Hugo should be interested*
*in this sort of thing.*
*I have had a long talk to him and tried to point out*
*some of the dangers into which he is running.*
*I hope I have convinced him,*
*but the matter will need careful watching*
*and so I am sure you will keep your eyes open*
*at home, just as I shall here.*

*Yours sincerely, Roy Hadwell.*

## There

If I got into trouble I was to go to him
and tell him everything.
It didn't matter if I was unhappy, or in love,
or wanted by the police. I could say,
'Daddy, I've killed a Chinaman'
and he'd see what he could do.

He gave me a knife for my birthday
and I cut my hand on it
and flung it away into the long grass,
running after it in vain
as it started to disappear.

It was easy to imagine myself
finding the knife and wearing it on a chain
the way he had shown me,
but not so easy when the grass had grown
and been cut many times,
the garden gone next door.

I must have been looking too far away
or I must have been looking too near.
A wealth of personal detail
accumulates in folders like a life of crime,
but nothing conclusive,
nothing to get arrested for.

# Snorkel

*To my Brother*

You carried the rattans and the towels.
I carried the windshield
and one of the old snorkels
with ping-pong balls for valves.

What happened to the other one
with yellow glass, the one that was dangerous?
We both wanted that one.
It didn't mist up. We slung ourselves

half way between heaven and earth
that summer—holding our breath
and diving for sand-dollars.
If we breathed out all the air in our lungs

we could grab another ten seconds
on the sea-bed. We spent half our lives
waiting for each other to come out of the water
so we could have our turn.

# New Ground

We played Scrabble wrong for years.
We counted the Double and Triple Word Scores
as often as we liked.
We had to move aside the letters
to see what colours they were on.

My father was out of work
and we were moving again. He stared at the board,
twisting his signet ring.
He liked adding 's' to a word
and scoring more points
than the person who thought of it.

He wanted 'chinas'. He said they were ornamental
bricks from Derbyshire, hand-painted.
He cheated from principle, to open up new ground
for his family. Not 'God feeds the ravens',
but *Mundum mea patria est*. We were stuck

at the end of a lane in Sussex
for two winters. My father threw down
his high-scoring spelling mistakes and bluffs
and started counting.
He would have walked all over us
if we'd let him have the last word—

'aw' as in 'Aw, hell!', 'ex' with the 'x' falling
on the last Triple Letter Score.
We made him take everything back.
What was left in his hand counted against him.

# Dégagé

He wanted me to look like him—well dressed,
but not too well.
I wanted to, but I was back to front,
tying and re-tying his ties
in front of the mirror, trying not to care
that they hung from my adam's apple like a noose
when I talked to girls.
Clothes were a kind of wit. You either
carried them off, or you looked ridiculous.
'Make a girl laugh,' said my father,
which I did. Whatever I put on
made me look even younger than my brother,
who was ten. I tried every combination
of cravat and cardigan in my efforts to look
natural, *dégagé*. I dug my hand
into the pocket of my flannels
and felt the little rolls of pocket dust
under my fingernails—and remained a virgin.

My father's forty-seven suits
awaiting his pleasure in a separate dressing room
were proof of his superior wit. Who else
had a white barathea dinner jacket
he never even wore, or turned-back cuffs
and no turn-ups on his trousers?
At fourteen I was nagging my grandmother
to make me shirts with fuller sleeves.
My jeans I wanted taken in and flared.
I was very keen on suede.
'You should be with someone a full minute
before you realize they're well-dressed,'
said my father. I imagined it dawning on people
in sixty seconds flat
that I was his equal at last.

'Suppose you realize before that?' I asked,
wriggling my toes in my chisel-toed chukka boots.
'Probably queer,' said my father.

# Making Friends with Ties

His khaki tie was perfectly knotted in wartime.
The tail was smartly plumped.
The dent became a groove
where it entered a sturdy, rectangular knot,
never a Windsor. This groove came out
in exactly the same place all his life,
like a grin, never in the middle,
but slightly to the left.
'You have to get it right first time,'
he told me, my first term at school,
'otherwise you go raving mad.'
I was so impressed by this
I didn't listen in class.
I made friends with people's ties, not them.
One day when I was drunk I told him,
'I don't like the groove!'
His face softened towards me for a moment.
'Don't you, dear boy? Well, I'm *delighted.*'

# Three Quarters

I wasn't happy with aspects of my case.
I shut myself in the bathroom,
a three-sided looking glass open like a book.
I couldn't understand my face. My nose stuck out.
I combed my hair down over my eyes
in search of a parting that would change all this.

I opened the mirror slowly, turning my head
from full to three-quarter face.
I wanted to stand three-quarters on to the world,
near the vanishing point.
I sat in front of the sunray lamp
with pennies in my eyes. I dyed my skin

a streaky, yellowish brown with permanganate of potash.
I must have grown up slowly
in that looking glass bathroom,
combing my hair straight down and pretending to wash.
I made myself dizzy raising my arms above my head
in a kind of surrender. No one else could get in.

# Early Work

When I came downstairs my hair looked extraordinary—
a turmoil of popular styles and prejudices,
stiff with unreality and fear.
My scalp stung from onsets of a steel flick-comb.
My parting was raw from realignment.
I'd reintroduced the casual look so many times
I'd forgotten what it was. The whole thing
looked like an instrument of self-torture
with a handle and a zip.

I made my entrance and everyone wanted to know
where I was off to looking like that.
My brother did a comb mime with his knife,
tongue hanging out, jacket pushed back like a Ted.
My father made me go upstairs and start again.
I'd been working on my hair for so long
I thought it was natural to have a whirlpool
on your head, or a ship. I couldn't grasp the fact
that my hair was my hair, nothing more.

# Raids on Lunch

Every lunchtime I came under threat
from my father's parting,
a venomous vapour trail
set at right angles to his profile.
I was the enemy,
po-faced and pale
and armed with a sort of quiff.
I had to make him laugh.
'Ett, ett,' he snapped,
shooting down a joke,
when I made the mistake
of pronouncing 'ate'
as if it rhymed with 'late'.
I hated the way his jaw went slack
as he calmly demolished me.
I couldn't resist
saying something tasteless
about the Royal Air Force,
having seen him disguised as a nun
in 'One of Our Aircraft is Missing'.
I should have run for cover.
Hooking a forefinger
over his much-admired nose
was the remains of my father's
camera-consciousness.
It meant he was critical:
the moment of sloth
before the nun takes off her head-dress
and opens fire on the Nazis.

# A Parting Shot

When I started going out
my father thought my hair should go straight back.
It grew straight forward.

He offered to wet it for me,
to train it back, like his. 'I used to have full lips
like yours when I was your age.'

We looked at each other
in the three-sided looking glass, ranks
of opposing profiles fanning out round the room.
His parting stood like a feather in his cap.

He laid his cigarette on the shelf
and started wetting my hair.
'For God's sake, GROW UP!' he shouted,
emptying the jug over my head.

# The Spring of Sheep

Pro-Plus Rapid Energy Tablets
gave me Extra Vitality
when I visited my girlfriend on her father's stud.
The double-backing local bus
took two hours to travel twenty miles.
When it passed our house
I nearly got off by mistake.
I noticed a roof I hadn't been on
and I wished I was up there with my gun.
My hands where shaking
as I thought of things to say:
how the enlargements had gone astray
and been pinned to the noticeboard,
how my tutor asked if it was Brigitte Bardot.
I practised laughing in the window of the bus,
but I laughed on the other side of my face
when I saw her riding her pony
in her Sloppy Joe.
We were sitting alone in the nursery,
waiting for her father's horse to appear on television.
My left hand felt numb,
but my right took leave of its senses
and set out for the unknown regions of her shoulders.
I watched through binoculars
as it lay there with altitude sickness.
If it was mine, how could I get it back in time
for dinner with her parents, bloodstock
and doping scandals? A gong
sounded somewhere in the house
and I leapt to my feet. Everyone was proud
of the gallant Citizen Roy
and my girlfriend ran over to the stables
to say goodnight. Head-over-heels with Pro-Plus,

I lay awake for hours, experiencing fierce
but tender feelings for the mattress
in a spare room hung with antique jigsaws:
'Les Generaux en herbe (The Future Generals)'
'Le Jeu de Balle (The Game of Balls)'
'Le Saut du Mouton (The Spring of Sheep)'.

## Sonny Jim In Love

They left me alone with the pens
and I have gone over my loved one's face
in ink, for something to do.
I wanted to see how she looked
telling me not to, so I let my hand
trail on her cheek like a hook.
Wasn't I her pet? Her little marmoset?
I traced a well-worn path
back and forth between her eyes
in search of crumbs.
I ran the gauntlet of her tantrums.

When she drew ahead of me
I scribbled for my life. Jagged lines
shot this way and that like looks
blurring her skin. Nervous attention
(glance towards) alternated rapidly
with nervous submission (glance away)
until I felt dizzy. I gave her
horn-rimmed spectacles, blacking them in
where her eyes accused me of
following her round the room. I broke a nib
crossing out her kindness to the dog.

I wasn't satisfied
till I had joined up her eyes and mouth
in a rough-hewn triangle,
a monkey-face. I watched a pen
snag the corner of her mouth, spattering
ink on my cuff. I went through
the paper and the paper beneath
in my efforts to make good.
When they asked me what I was drawing in my book
I told them everyone looked like that
by the time I had scribbled my gaze on them.

# A Touch of '8' for Debonair Roles

Spots of Leichner '5' and '9'
alternated round his face like warpaint
when we talked about my writing. 'One blockbuster
and you'll never have to work again', he told me,
rubbing the red and white markings down to a tan
for drawing room comedy. He opened the window
onto an area where some old overcoats had been left
hanging on railings. 'Look at that!' he whispered,
'The Tramp's Cloakroom. Now there's a subject for you.'
We stared into the night. 'They'll be gone by October',
he said, 'but where to, that's what we'll never know.'

# A Start in Life

One such paragon, able to play anything from cuckolded husbands to dainty blackmailers without his assumed character being allowed to affect his performance in any way, was Hugh Williams, at once heroic yet vulnerable. He watched me rehearse my Dutch priest, then he came up to me and asked what I was going to do in this scene. 'I don't know, Mr Williams,' I said, adding hopefully, 'I thought I'd do nothing.'
'O no you don't,' he said, a trace of hardness entering his voice, 'I'm doing nothing in this scene.'

Peter Ustinov, *Dear Me*

Of course I wanted to be an actor. I had the gold chain
like Alain Delon. I could lift one eyebrow.
I didn't wear any socks.
I came home from France
with a brush-cut and a sketch of myself
and my father said 'WHAT ARE YOU GOING TO DO?'
'I'll let it grow out', I wanted to say.
'I don't like it any more.'
Wine was his vision of my future, followed by hotels.
'You get your own set of professional carving knives
from somewhere in Smithfield.
It's an investment for life. A form of security.'

I wish I had them now. Work had this mad
glint in its eye, which made me look away.
I practised my draw in the mirror.
'The honeymoon's over', said my father.
'I don't care what you do
so long as it isn't a politician, a poof or a tenor.'
I made a face, scanning the South Downs
for something easier.

On a good day I could see the Chanctonbury Ring
outlined against the horizon.
'I want to be an actor', I said.
My father slapped his knee.

'No you don't', he shouted. 'You don't give a damn
about the theatre, or me. You write poetry.
When I was your age I'd seen every play in London.
I read plays for fun. I wanted passionately to act.
Can you say that?' His widow's peak
was like a judge's black cap as he laid down the law.
'Acting's showing off', I said to the downs.
'It's the perfect cover for people like us
who can't do anything else.
It's better than nothing anyway.'
I walked in the garden, shaking one of his collars
till it fell to pieces in my hand.

I dried my eyes, but I never did land
the job he was looking for. I stayed where I was,
waiting for a last call to find me
putting on make-up in my dressing room—
'Five minutes please, Mr Williams'—
as if I could still go on
and make a start in life. I see the downs even now
like a backdrop to the scene.
I put on different clothes and I see myself in action.
It feels like drawing a gun in slow motion
over and over again. I have the gold chain
like Alain Delon. I can lift one eyebrow.

# Death Of An Actor

*i.m. Hugh Williams 1904–1969*

1.

Now that I am cold
Now that I look like him
I put on this warm grey suit of wool
In sympathy with my father.

Now that I'm alone
Now that I have come to this nice
Indifference
I sweep my hair straight back
The way he wore it during his life
And after he was dead
His fierce forehead
Still doubting the intelligence
Of those who approached where he lay.

2.

Now that he is dead
Now that he is remembered
Unfavourably by some
For phrases too well cut
To fit their bonhomie
I wonder what he was like
This stiff theatrical man
With his air of sealed regret.
'I'd have made a first class tramp',
He told me once,
'If I'd had more money.'

Now that it is late
Now that it is too late
For filial piety

I can but thank him for
His bloody-mindedness.
Face expressionless with pain
He ordered me a suit in Savile Row
The very day he took
The last plunge backwards
Into secrecy and sweat.
'O Dad, can dead men swim?'

3.
Gold on the doorstep, whose steps
Nag the sand-drifts.
Gold in the spittoon.

My father would sit on the steps
Emptying his shoe.
Pitchers of sand on each step.

If they went on, they would lead
To an ocean. Gold in a silver spoon.
My father's throat torn to sand.

4.
Our first Christmas after the war
A triangular package
Arrived from his producer.

'Greetings from Emile Littler'
Said the message printed on the bar
Of a single coathanger.

5.
Now that I have tucked myself in
To this deep basement calm
And the windows are sealed for winter,
Now that my life is organized

To absorb the shock
Of looking back at it,
I understand why he put such vast whiskies
Into the hands of his enemies
And I take back what I said.

Now that I am grown
Now I have children of my own
To offer me their own
Disappointed obedience
I feel for him.
Our children left us both
Because we sat so still
And were too wise for them
When they told us their best jokes.

6.
My father was last to leave the stage
In *The Cherry Orchard* in 1966.
He said to his bookshelves,
'My friends, my dear good friends,
How can I be silent?
How can I refrain from expressing, as I leave,
The thoughts that overwhelm my being?'
His sister was calling him,
'The station . . . the train. Uncle,
Shouldn't we be going?'

7.
The recording starts too late
To drown the sound of wheels. A little screen
Jerks upwards and the coffin
Wobbles towards us on rollers, like a diving board.
This is my father's curtain call. His white-ringed eyes
Flicker to the gallery as he bows to us. He bows

To his leading lady, then steps back again,
Rejoining hands with the cast.

In the dressing-room afterwards
He pours us all champagne:
'It's like a madhouse here. We're staffed by chumps.
The stage manager thinks the entire production
Stems from his control panel, like a cremation.
He's never heard of laughs. As for the set,
Tom says it's the old Jermyn Street Turkish Baths
Painted shit. Let's hope it doesn't run.'

8.
Now that he is gone
Now that we have followed him this far
To a push-button crematorium
In unknown Golders Green
I think how near he seems, compared to formerly,
His head thrown back like that
Almost in laughter.
I used to watch him making up
In an underground dressing-room,
His head thrown back that way:
A cream and then a bright red spot
Rubbed down to a healthy tan.

Now that he is gone
Now that we have seen his coffin
Roll through those foul flaps
And a curtain ring down for the last time
On a sizeable man
I remember how calm he remained
Throughout the final scene,
Sitting bolt upright
On a windswept platform.
'The coldest place in the south of England',

He used to say—off on tour again
In one of his own plays.

9.
Now that he has returned to that station
Where the leave-train is waiting
Blacked-out and freezing,
The smell of whisky lingers on my breath,
A patch of blue sky
Stings like a slap in the face.

Now that he isn't coming down
On the midnight train tonight, or any night,
I realize how far
Death takes men on from where they were
And yet how soon
It brings them back again.

10.
Now that I'm the same age
As he was during the war,
Now that I hold him up like a mirror
To look over my shoulder,
I'm given to wondering
What manner of man it was
Who walked in on us that day
In his final uniform.
A soldier with two families?
An actor without a career?
'You didn't know who on earth I was,' he told me.
'You just cried and cried.'

Now that he has walked out again
Leaving me no wiser,
Now that I'm sitting here like an actor
Waiting to go on,

I wish I could see again
That rude, forgiving man from World War II
And hear him goading me.
Dawdling in peacetime,
Not having to fight in my lifetime, left alone
To write poetry on the dole and be happy,
I'm given to wondering
What manner of man I might be.

# Unfinished Poem

When he falls asleep tonight, I'll sit still
with the stuffed crocodile, wondering what to do.
Have another shot from the bottle?
Or go upstairs and look for evidence of myself?
I've seen it all before—the toilet case
of film star cigarette cards, the bundles of old
theatre programmes, unfinished albums
from Eden Roc and The Garden of Allah.

My father's elevators perish in a drawer.
His false beard weeps to itself.
Only his autograph, scrawled impatiently
on hundreds of pin-up photographs,
looks anything like mine, so patiently copied from it.
When I burst in on his sleep
with a head hollowed out of a turnip
swinging from a broom, the villain Steerforth
smiles at my innocence, Mr Darcy looks at me
through his eyeglass and asks if I've been drinking.

# Sonny Jim's House

The cistern groans under a new pressure.
Little known taps are being turned on
in obscure regions of the house,
cutting off the water for his tea.
Jim forwards her mail to the garden, laughing
because he has hidden the marmalade.

At nine they both stay home and do nothing,
out of work. The ring in the bath and the
hacked loaf prove he is on the track
of his elusive wife. Her movements displace
the usual volume of elegant soft-porn: face-
creams and cigarettes. Now Jim has razor-burn.

By the end of the afternoon he will have taken
a thousand pairs of sex-oriented shoes
back to her dressing-room. Jim swears
he can still see the funny side of life
in a halfway house where even the shoes
exist in limbo and the hand-rail is loose.

He puts his ear to the door of the study,
rushes in, sees the back of his head.
This is where he sits alone, in coffee-shock,
making lists of women. Photos of his wife
line the walls, reminding him of her.
The cupboard is open. He can't decide what to wear.

When the front door bangs he imagines his wife
has gone out and runs upstairs to look at
her clothes. Blocked by her breakfast tray,
he comes back down again, asking himself
whether the hall is part of the original house
or something to do with the street.

Jim thinks there are two houses here,
each one overlapping the other, like towels,
the spiral stair acting as a kind of hinge
for correct and incorrect behaviour. He stands
for hours on end, rolling his eyes
in soapy water dreams, unable to go up or down.

# Speech Day

*To Neil Rennie*

It comes at you out of nowhere, with 'Hello, Muggins!
You still here?' or 'Myers was travelling through
Europe on his way to Strasbourg', the sense of time
unravelling without you, the possibilities
of what might happen if you did nothing
running neck and neck with your attention span
in a sack race for the dead. It's too like life:
unwarranted enthusiasm somehow using itself up
in time for the end to happen, as when, on Speech Day,
the Head Boy comes to the front of the stage
to thank the staff for making it all possible
and us for bearing with him, in spite of the seating.

# A Picture of a Girl in a Bikini

I look over the bannisters and see, far down,
Miss Pyke taking Callover. I push my feet
into a pair of Cambridge house shoes
half my size and shuffle downstairs.
When I answer my name there is a long silence,
then Miss Pyke asks me where I've been.
I tell her I was reading a book
and didn't notice the time.

I see I have a smaller desk this term
as a punishment for being late.
I have to sit sideways, facing Armitage,
who eats little pieces of blotting paper
dipped in ink. When the bell goes
I barge off down Lower Corridor
with my head down and my elbows out,
knocking everyone flying.

Hurrah! There's a letter for me today.
I'd rather have a parcel, but I'm always happy
when I see the familiar blue envelope
propped on the mantelpiece
on the other side of School Hall.
I don't open it straight away, of course.
I shove it in my pocket
and read it later, like a man.

I'm standing outside the Headmaster's Study
waiting for the green light to come on.
Either I've failed Common Entrance
or my parents have died. When I go in
he's sitting at his desk, staring out the window.
For a long time we watch Sgt. Burrows
pushing his marker round Long Field,
Mr Harvey taking fielding practice.

The Headmaster pulls his writing case towards him
and opens it with his paper knife.
Inside is the worst news in the world,
my copy of Man Junior with a picture of a girl
in a bikini playing with a beach ball.
I must have left it under my mattress.
The Headmaster looks at me in disbelief
and asks, 'What is the meaning of this?'

# No Particular Place To Go

O'Sullivan's Record Exchange
in the Peskett Street Market
was out of bounds to Lower Boys
on account of Miss O'Sullivan's taste
in music. We used to jive
in the listening booths
when she turned the volume up for us,
knowing we wouldn't buy.
It was the best she could do.
You couldn't hear that kind of thing
any other way in 1956. The overloaded wires
must have set fire to the partitioning.
They had to throw hundreds of
twisted 78's out onto the pavement.

O'Sullivan's Record Exchange,
its record-covered walls suspended
in their own flames, still seems to welcome me
with all my favourite tunes,
and Miss O'Sullivan
moving her arms over the turntables
like one who heals. When I'm caught
loitering in the new car park
off Peskett Street ten years from now
and taken for questioning, I'll know
what to expect: 'Look here old boy,
the past is out of bounds, you should know that.'
'But sir,' I'll say, 'where else is there to go
on these half-holidays?'

# Returning Soldier

He must be standing by a window, looking out
on a backdrop of Regent's Park. The sound
of carriage wheels on gravel, a woman's laugh.
As the lights come up, he moves to centre stage
to check his tie: the perfect kid-gloved cad.

In a government-issue busman's overcoat,
long in the sleeve,
a white arm-band for 'officer material',
he looks more like the wronged husband of the piece.
'Don't just do something, sit there'
was the word of command
to the men guarding Staines Railway Bridge
during the Phoney War.

*As the dust settled I could see your father*
*stretched out beside the road, clutching a map.*
*I lifted him up*
*and propped him against the side of the jeep.*
*'Come on, sir' I said. 'Have a cigarette, sir.*
*You always have a cigarette when you wake up.'*
*He didn't get the picture at first.*
*He thought he had trodden in something cold*
*and fallen over backwards.*
*'I got my bastard left foot wet', he said.*

Now that he's walking towards me in long shot,
limping a little from the war,
Now that he pauses for a moment in close-up,
lighting a cigarette,
I find myself playing the kid-gloved cad
to his returning soldier.
I'm sitting on the edge of my seat
to find out what I say.

# Going Round Afterwards

His face was orange.
His widow's peak had been blacked in.
I knew it was him,
because he didn't speak.
'Congratulations!' I said.
'I didn't know you could cry.'
His dresser was holding
a pair of check trousers
underneath his chin. He let the legs
drop through a coathanger
and smiled at me deafly.
'It's just a trick', said my father.
'Anyone can do it.'
I stood there with my drink,
feeling the ingenious glamour
of being cramped, the mild delinquency
of things behind curtains—
shirts and cardigans
that should have been at home.
Did I have the guts?
And did you have to want it all that much
in order to go on?
His face came up from the wash basin
white and unwell again,
a trace of make-up underneath his ears.
His dresser was handing him
another pair of trousers,
holding them up off the floor
as my father stepped into them.

# Now That I Hear Trains

Now that I hear trains
whistling out of Paddington on their way to Wales,
I like to think of him, as young as he was then,
running behind me along the sand,
holding my saddle steady
and launching me off on my own.

Now that I look unlike
the boy on the brand new bike
who wobbled away down the beach,
I hear him telling me: 'Keep pedalling, keep pedalling.'
When I looked over my shoulder
he was nowhere to be seen.